Prefixes are small letter groups added **before** base or root words. A prefix changes the meaning of the base or root word.

Example: Tina had to **repaint** the fence every summer.

The prefix **re** means **"again."** By adding "re" to the word "paint," the word is changed to mean "to paint again." The prefix **de** means **"from."**

Fill in the blank in each sentence with the prefix "de" or "re."

1. The teacher asked him to _____ **word** the sentences in his story.

2. He will _____ **design** the wing on his model airplane.

3. After she had corrected her mistakes, Amanda decided to _____ **copy** her paper.

4. Did you remember to _____ **frost** the meat you removed from the freezer?

5. The people in the country tried to _____ **throne** the king.

6. Jim's teacher gave him a ____ **merit** because he was chewing gum in school.

7. Sally always _____ **views** her spelling list the night before the test.

8. The train was _____ **railed** in the accident.

9. The detective will _____ **code** the secret message.

10. Dad wants to _____ **new** his subscription to the sports magazine.

11. Please _____ **fill** my glass with lemonade.

12. After being closed for several months, the movie theater will_____ **open** this Saturday.

13. We listened to the story as it was _____ **told** by the author of the book.

Decide if the missing prefix for each word is "de" or "re." Write the correct prefix on the line.

The prefix **de** means **"from."**   The prefix **re** means **"again."**

1. _____code

2. _____turn

3. _____word

4. _____new

5. _____frost

6. _____throne

7. _____trace

8. _____store

9. _____view

10. _____fill

Each of the words in the first column has a prefix and a base word. Print the prefix for each word in the second column. Print the base word in the third column. The first one has been done for you.

Prefix   Base Word

1. recopy _____re_____   _____copy_____

2. defrost _____   _____

3. refill _____   _____

4. redo _____   _____

5. repay _____   _____

6. decode _____   _____

7. relive _____   _____

8. reload _____   _____

9. deform _____   _____

10. reclaim _____   _____

11. reset _____   _____

For each problem, fill in the prefix "dis" or "un" to form a new word.

The prefix **dis** means **"opposite."**	The prefix **un** means **"not."**

1. _____like

2. _____do

3. _____believe

4. _____scramble

5. _____prepared

6. _____even

7. _____appear

8. _____agree

9. _____easy

10. _____real

11. _____continue

12. _____connect

13. _____pack

14. _____honest

15. _____clear

16. _____lock

17. _____obey

18. _____ earned

19. _____place

20. _____happy

21. _____fair

Each of the words below has a prefix and a base word. For each word, write the prefix on the left side and the base word on the right side. The first one has been done for you.

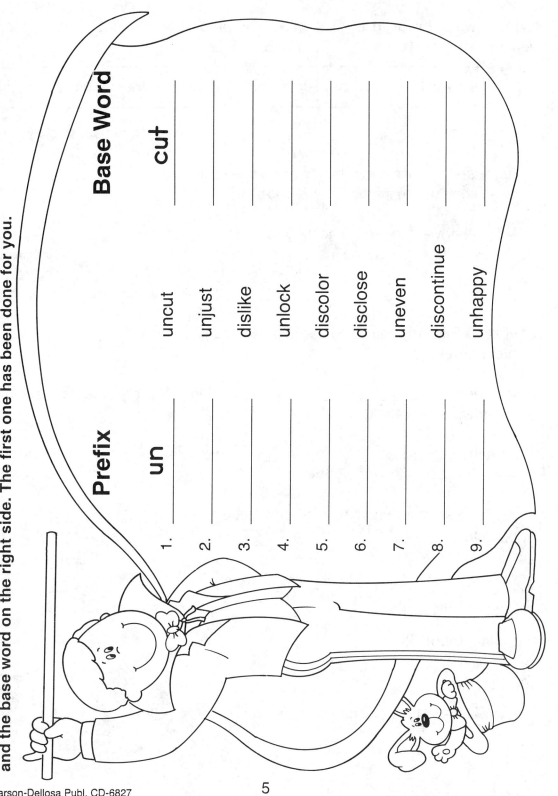

	Prefix		Base Word
1. uncut	un		cut
2. unjust			
3. dislike			
4. unlock			
5. discolor			
6. disclose			
7. uneven			
8. discontinue			
9. unhappy			

5

Add the prefix "in" or "pre" to each word in parentheses. Print the new word on the line in the sentence.

The prefix **in** means **"not"** or **"into."**   The prefix **pre** means **"before."**

1. Maria had to _____ for her gymnastics class. **(pay)**

2. Because Sara has fair skin, she always uses sunblock as a _____ when she goes to the beach. **(caution)**

3. My mother went to the elementary school to _____ my sister for kindergarten. **(register)**

4. We saw a _____ for the new adventure movie. **(view)**

5. I had to finish my homework last night because it was _____ . **(complete)**

6. We had to _____ my soccer shirt in laundry detergent to remove the grass stain. **(soak)**

7. Anthony decided to _____ the potatoes so they would be ready when his guests arrived. **(cook)**

8. We were amazed when the magician made the rabbit _____ . **(visible)**

9. Mark was excited because his soccer team

   was playing at the _____

   arena. **(door)**

10. Our class went to see the _____

   dinosaur exhibit at the museum. **(historic)**

Circle the base word in each word.

1. p r e s o a k	2. i n v i s i b l e
3. u n c l e a n	4. u n c l e a r
5. u n s a f e	6. u n f a i r
7. u n h a p p y	8. u n r e a l
9. u n k i n d	10. u n e v e n
11. p r e t e s t	12. d i s c o n n e c t
13. u n f a s t e n	14. r e f i l l

Each of the words in the first column has a prefix and a base word. Print the prefix for each word in the second column. Print the base word in the third column. The first one has been done for you.

	Prefix	Base Word
1. incorrect	in	correct
2. insincere	_____	_____
3. unclear	_____	_____
4. uncut	_____	_____
5. refresh	_____	_____
6. discolor	_____	_____
7. incomplete	_____	_____
8. research	_____	_____
9. unhappy	_____	_____
10. disconnect	_____	_____
11. retell	_____	_____

Suffixes are letter groups that are added to the end of base or root words. Suffixes often add information to the meaning of words.

Example: The bubble gum was **sugarless.**

The suffix **less** means **"without"** and changes the meaning of the base word "sugar."

The suffix **ness** means **"state or quality of."**

Fill in the blank on each fish with the suffix "less" or "ness."

1. use _____

2. rest _____

3. good _____

4. fruit _____

5. like _____

6. thought _____

7. speech _____

8. care _____

9. tough _____

10. foolish _____

11. blame _____

12. end _____

13. worth _____

14. playful _____

15. hope _____

16. dark _____

Complete the word in each sentence by adding the suffix "ly" or "less."

> The suffix **less** means **"without."**   The suffix **ly** means **"in what manner."**

1. The lemonade was **complete** _____ gone by the end of the day.

2. She poured the drinks **careful**_____ into the glasses.

3. We knew it was **hope** _____ to try to make enough lemonade for the whole school.

4. The sun was shining and it was a **cloud** _____ day.

5. The dog was sitting **motion**_____ by the lemonade stand.

6. The lemonade was **light** _____ sweetened.

7. He drank the entire glass of lemonade very **quick** _____ .

8. We knew it was **sense** _____ to think that the boy wouldn't want a drink.

9. Helen **swift** _____ came to our aid when we asked her to help us.

10. Jack became very **rest** _____ sitting behind the lemonade stand.

11. The lemonade stand was **entire** _____ Jane's idea.

12. The lemonade sale was **high** _____ successful.

13. We **rapid** _____ began making more lemonade to fill the pitchers.

14. Jim is **slow** _____ squeezing all of the lemons.

15. We put all the cups away **neat** _____ .

The suffix "less" or "ness" can be added to each of the words on the word list. Decide which suffix to add to each word and print the new word on the pencil under the correct suffix. When a word ends in "y," change the "y" to "i" before adding a suffix.

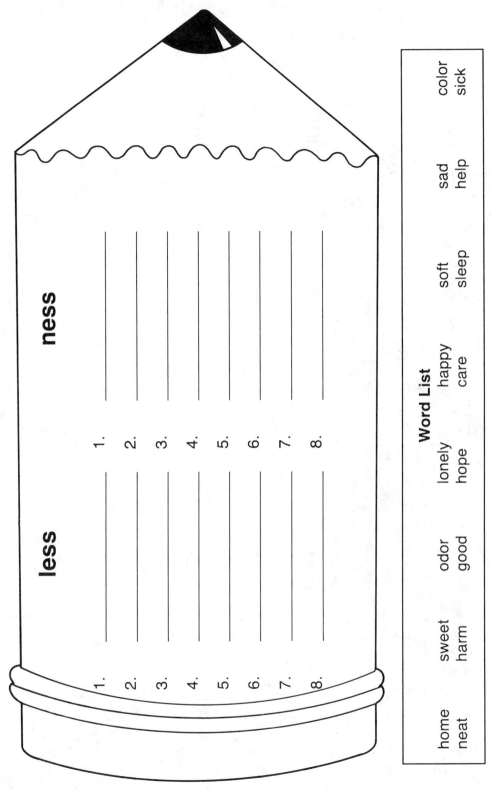

less

1. _____
2. _____
3. _____
4. _____
5. _____
6. _____
7. _____
8. _____

ness

1. _____
2. _____
3. _____
4. _____
5. _____
6. _____
7. _____
8. _____

Word List

home	sweet	odor	lonely	happy	soft	sad	color
neat	harm	good	hope	care	sleep	help	sick

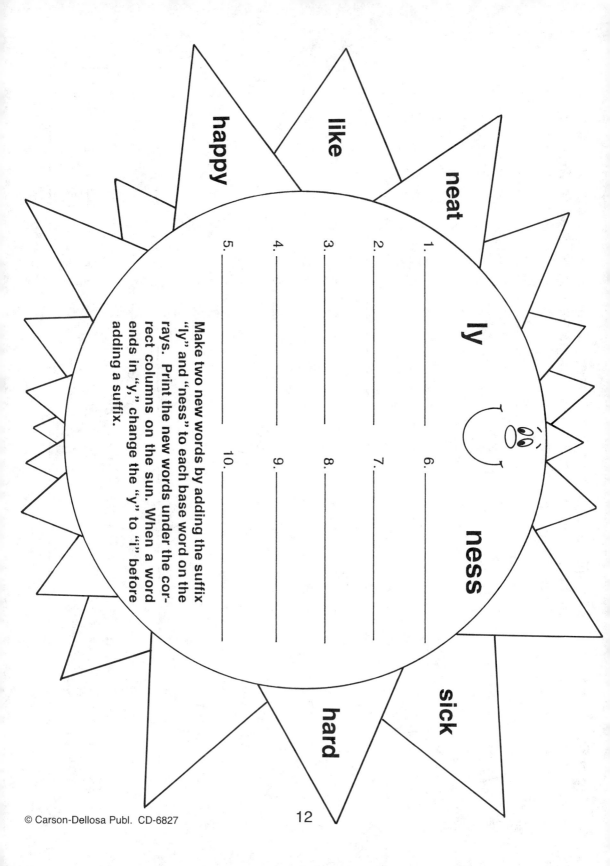

happy

like

neat

ly

ness

sick

hard

1. _____

2. _____

3. _____

4. _____

5. _____

6. _____

7. _____

8. _____

9. _____

10. _____

Make two new words by adding the suffix "ly" and "ness" to each base word on the rays. Print the new words under the correct columns on the sun. When a word ends in "y," change the "y" to "i" before adding a suffix.

Each word on the first teapot can have the suffix "able" added to it. Print the new words on the second teapot.

The suffix **able** means "**inclined to.**"

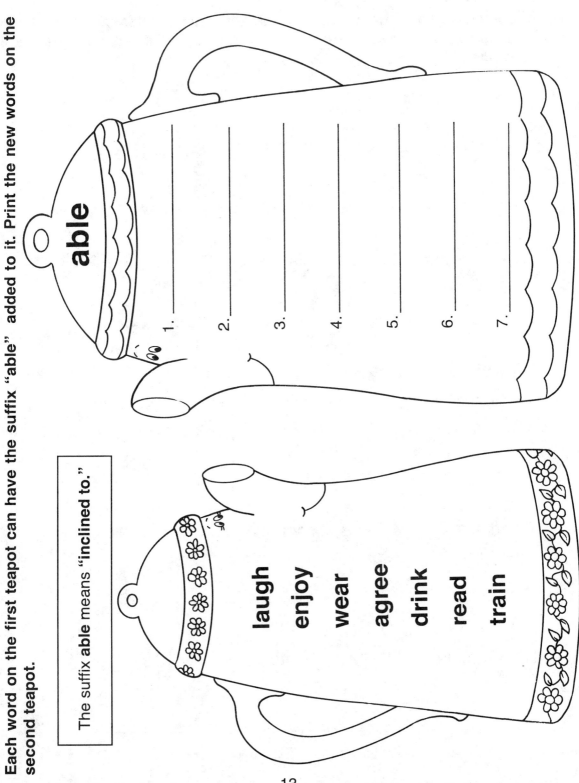

able

1. _____
2. _____
3. _____
4. _____
5. _____
6. _____
7. _____

laugh

enjoy

wear

agree

drink

read

train

The words below have the suffix "er" added to them. Decide what the base words are and print them on the lines. Be careful. Some of the base words were changed when the suffixes were added.

1. batter

2. singer

3. jogger

4. hitter

5. popper

6. caller

7. skier

8. baker

9. shopper

10. walker

11. drummer

12. hunter

13. digger

The suffix "ed" has been added to the base words to form the words listed below. Decide what the base words are and print them on the lines. Be careful. Some of the base words were changed when the suffixes were added.

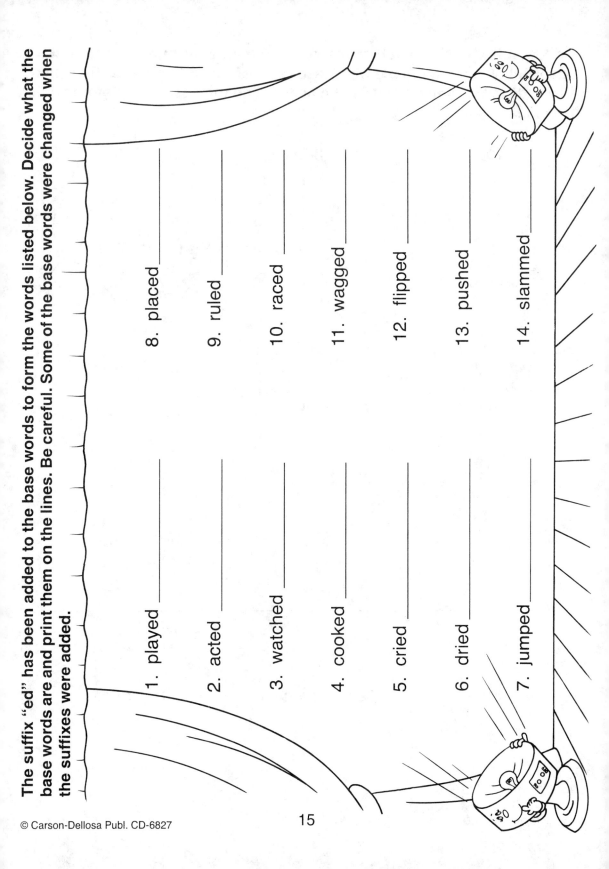

1. played _____

2. acted _____

3. watched _____

4. cooked _____

5. cried _____

6. dried _____

7. jumped _____

8. placed _____

9. ruled _____

10. raced _____

11. wagged _____

12. flipped _____

13. pushed _____

14. slammed _____

Add the suffix "ed" to each of the words. When a word ends with a single consonant, you must double the consonant before adding the suffix. When a word ends in "e," you must drop the final "e" on the base word before adding the suffix.

1. trot

2. juggle

3. jump

4. like

5. touch

6. yell

7. walk

8. grin

9. jog

10. nap

11. drum

12. crush

13. rain

Read the words on the worms. The suffix "ing" has been added to each base word. Cut out the bodies and paste them under the correct base words.

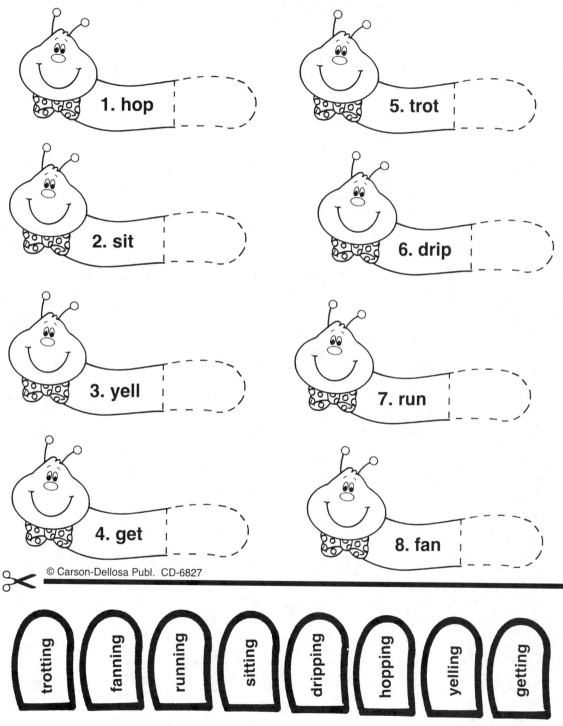

1. hop

5. trot

2. sit

6. drip

3. yell

7. run

4. get

8. fan

trotting | fanning | running | sitting | dripping | hopping | yelling | getting

Complete each sentence by adding the suffix "ing" to the word in parentheses. When a word ends in "e," you must drop the "e" before adding the suffix.

1. We go ice _____ on the pond every winter. **(skate)**

2. Tad's red soccer jersey was _____ because it has been washed many times. **(fade)**

3. My sister is _____ decorations for my birthday party. **(make)**

4. Sean and his family are _____ to Florida this summer. **(drive)**

5. Shannon and Leslie are _____ their bicycles on the path. **(ride)**

6. Because of poor business, the store is _____ permanently. **(close)**

7. Ted is_____ all of the old newspapers in his neighborhood for recycling. **(save)**

8. Ashley is _____ a special cake for the graduation party. **(bake)**

9. Zach is _____ several classes at the university this fall. **(take)**

10. Sally was_____ to be finished with her homework by dinnertime. **(hope)**

11. Lauren is _____ the picture from the book. **(trace)**

12. Matthew is having trouble _____ his new kitten. **(name)**

Write the prefix "pre," "mis," or "re" on each blank to form a new word.

A.

_____ read

B.

_____ fill

C.

_____ build

D.

_____ write

E.

_____ call

F.

_____ spell

G.

_____ behave

H.

_____ heat

I.

_____ new

J.

_____ seal

K.

_____ school

L.

_____ lead

Complete each sentence using one of the new words above.

1. My glass is empty. Would you please _____ it?

2. If you want to pass the test, you must _____ these chapters.

3. Do not let Sandy's advice _____ you.

4. Please _____ these books when you go to the library.

5. To keep the cookies fresh, please _____ the bag.

6. Tim's paper was difficult to read, so he had to _____ it.

7. Please don't _____ while visiting your aunt.

8. Check your paper to make sure you didn't _____ any words.

9. The neighbors helped Mr. Gray _____his barn after the fire.

If the bold suffix has been correctly added to the word, color the watermelon slice red.

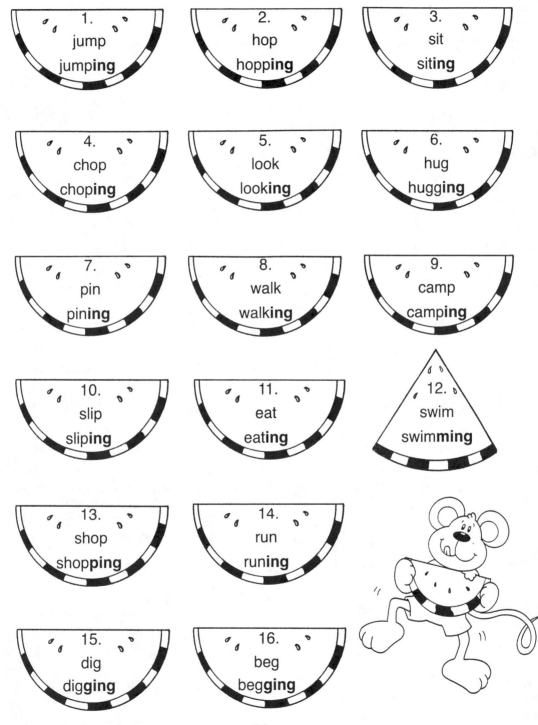

1. jump
jump**ing**

2. hop
hopp**ing**

3. sit
sit**ing**

4. chop
chop**ing**

5. look
look**ing**

6. hug
hugg**ing**

7. pin
pin**ing**

8. walk
walk**ing**

9. camp
camp**ing**

10. slip
slip**ing**

11. eat
eat**ing**

12. swim
swim**ming**

13. shop
shopp**ing**

14. run
run**ing**

15. dig
dig**ging**

16. beg
begg**ing**

21

Write "un," "dis," or "de" in each blank to form a new word.

A.

_____ usual

B.

_____ agree

C.

_____ continue

D.

_____ frost

E.

_____ safe

F.

_____ lock

G.

_____ honest

H.

_____ even

I.

_____ true

Complete each sentence using one of the new words above.

1. You must _____ the car windows to melt the ice.

2. Riding on the handlebars of a bike is _____ .

3. I had to _____ the front door so Sam could come in the house.

4. The company will _____ the product you recently bought.

5. Susan was _____ when she cheated on the test.

6. We were disappointed when we discovered the rumor about the concert was

   _____ .

7. People sometimes argue when they _____ .

8. The two pieces of yarn I cut were _____ .

9. Do not _____ the chain on your bicycle until you are ready to leave.

10. It was _____ for Justin not to eat breakfast before leaving for school.

Complete each word using the suffix "less" or "ness."

1. care _____

2. sad_____

3. use _____

4. neat _____

5. soft_____

6. rest _____

7. hard_____

8. home _____

9. hope _____

10. dark _____

11. thank _____

12. good _____

13. quick _____

14. sad _____

15. thought _____

16. shy _____

Write the suffix "able," "ful," or "ly" in each blank to form a new word.

A.
enjoy_____

B.
near_____

C.
move_____

D.
thank_____

E.
safe_____

F.
pain_____

G.
help_____

H.
drink_____

I.
care_____

Complete each sentence using one of the new words above.

1. My brother has a toy robot that has _____ arms.

2. My family was _____ that no one was hurt in the fire.

3. Susan said her broken leg was very _____.

4. Don't stop now! You are _____ finished.

5. Riding a bike_____ will prevent accidents.

6. When you wash the dishes, you are being _____.

7. Do not use the water from the well. It is not _____.

8. Please be _____ when using sharp scissors.

9. Alex finds swimming to be an _____ hobby.

10. The bee sting on my leg is very _____.

11. After the boat capsized, we were able to swim _____ to shore.

Complete each word using the suffix "ed." Remember, if a word ends in "e," you only add a "d."

1.

want_____

2.

save_____

3.

snow_____

4.

like_____

5.

use_____

6.

talk_____

7.

wipe_____

8.

bake_____

9.

share_____

10.

burn_____

11.

fill_____

12.

mail_____

13.

rain_____

Color the star blue if a silent "e" was dropped before adding "ing" to the word.

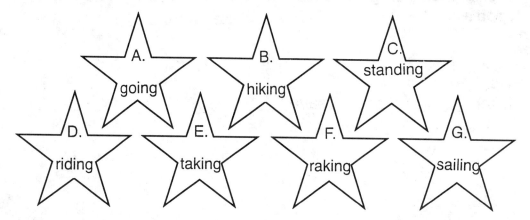

A. going
B. hiking
C. standing
D. riding
E. taking
F. raking
G. sailing

On the blank, write the correct form of the verb for each sentence.

1. We are _____ on a vacation in three weeks. **(go)**

2. Do you want to go _____ with us? **(hike)**

3. Kenny has been _____ for his dog for an hour. **(look)**

4. Bob is _____ leaves with his sister. **(rake)**

5. We have been _____ in line for five minutes. **(stand)**

6. Have you ever gone _____ on the lake? **(sail)**

7. I am _____ my lunch to school today. **(take)**

8. Kelly is _____ her new bicycle. **(ride)**

Color the whistle blue if you would add "ed" to the word. Color the whistle red if you would change the "y" to" i" and add "ed."

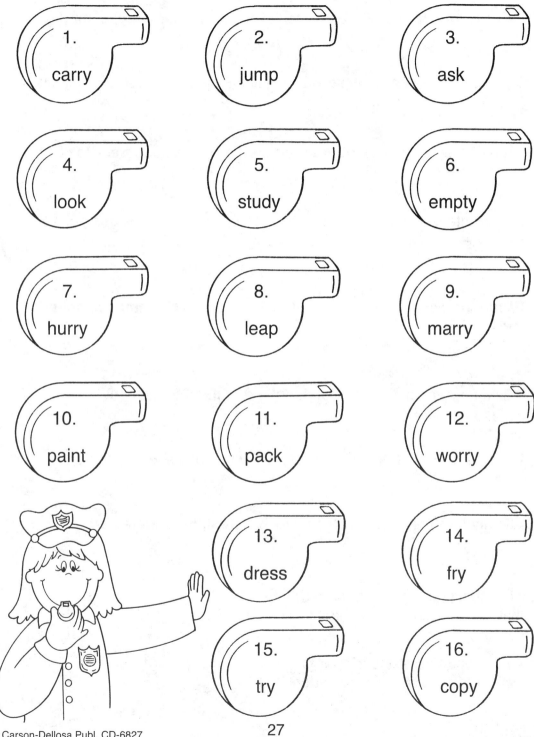

1. carry

2. jump

3. ask

4. look

5. study

6. empty

7. hurry

8. leap

9. marry

10. paint

11. pack

12. worry

13. dress

14. fry

15. try

16. copy

Circle the word that correctly completes each sentence.

1. One day Wendy and Wilma decided to go **(camp, camping, camped)**.

2. They **(pack, packing, packed)** everything they would need on their bikes.

3. Then off they rode to **(hunt, hunting, hunted)** for a good place to camp.

4. Finally, after looking a long time, they **(pick, picking, picked)** a great campsite.

5. Wendy lost control of her bike and went **(splash, splashing, splashed)** into a pond.

6. Wilma ran over and quickly **(pull, pulling, pulled)** Wendy out.

7. Wendy's hat was **(fill, filling, filled)** with water and even a little fish.

8. After that they both sat down on a rock to **(rest, resting, rested)**.

9. After going **(fish, fishing, fished)**, they cooked supper over the fire.

10. Wendy and Wilma hoped their fun would never **(end, ending, ended)**.

Write the suffix "ing" or "ed" on each line. Then find and circle each new word in the puzzle below.

1. Bill **knock** _____ on the door before he went in.

2. I am going **fish**_____ with my grandfather on Saturday.

3. Mary's family and mine are going **camp** _____ this weekend.

4. Susan is **dish** _____ out the ice cream.

5. Are you still **hunt** _____ for your wallet?

6. The children **toss** _____ the ball to each other.

O	T	C	L	L	P	E	L	D
B	N	A	P	G	T	F	E	I
T	E	M	B	R	A	H	M	S
U	Z	P	C	M	F	R	T	H
P	X	I	F	O	S	B	A	I
H	U	N	T	I	N	G	K	N
L	K	G	O	M	R	N	D	G
D	N	N	S	K	R	I	E	H
R	O	N	S	L	Z	S	H	E
H	C	T	E	T	F	S	S	Y
T	K	R	D	I	G	O	A	Q
R	E	K	Z	S	H	R	L	P
M	D	A	B	G	F	C	P	A
F	I	S	H	I	N	G	S	V

Complete each sentence by adding the correct suffix to the word in parentheses.

1. Ben _____ four miles today. **(jog)**

2. Sue is _____ the finish line. **(cross)**

3. Mark is _____ the baseball. **(bat)**

4. Jeff _____ his knee as he slid into third base. **(skin)**

5. Jim _____ the football over the goal post. **(kick)**

6. Because of the accident, the judge is _____ the race. **(stop)**

7. Ed was _____ from ear to ear as he received the first place ribbon. **(grin)**

8. The race horse _____ around the track. **(trot)**

9. Tina, Jerry, and Marcia are _____ to school every day this week. **(walk)**

10. The runner _____ over the hurdles and ran around the track. **(jump)**

11. Sally had _____ all of the dishes by the time we got home. **(wash)**

12. The new store will be _____ this week. **(open)**

13. The team is _____ a game tonight at the field. **(play)**

14. The coach was _____ out instructions from the sidelines. **(call)**

Pull-Out Answer Key

Page 1: 1. reword; 2. redesign; 3. recopy; 4. defrost; 5. dethrone; 6. demerit; 7. reviews; 8. derailed; 9. decode; 10. renew; 11. refill; 12. reopen; 13. retold

Page 2: 1. decode; 2. return; 3. reword; 4. renew; 5. defrost; 6. dethrone; 7. retrace; 8. restore; 9. review; 10. refill

Page 3: 1. re copy; 2. de frost; 3. re fill; 4. re do; 5. re pay; 6. de code; 7. re live; 8. re load; 9. de form; 10. re claim; 11. re set

Page 4: 1. dislike; 2. undo; 3. disbelieve; 4. unscramble; 5. unprepared; 6. uneven; 7. disappear; 8. disagree; 9. uneasy; 10. unreal; 11. discontinue; 12. disconnect; 13. unpack; 14. dishonest; 15. unclear; 16. unlock; 17. disobey; 18. unearned; 19. displace; 20. unhappy; 21. unfair

Page 5: 1. un cut; 2. un just; 3. dis like; 4. un lock; 5. dis color; 6. dis close; 7. un even; 8. dis continue; 9. un happy

Page 6: 1. prepay; 2. precaution; 3. preregister; 4. preview; 5. incomplete; 6. presoak; 7. precook; 8. invisible; 9. indoor; 10. prehistoric

Page 7: 1. presoak; 2. invisible; 3. unclean; 4. unclear; 5. unsafe; 6. unfair; 7. unhappy; 8. unreal; 9. unkind; 10. uneven; 11. pretest; 12. disconnect; 13. unfasten; 14. refill

Page 8: 1. in correct; 2. in sincere; 3. un clear; 4. un cut; 5. re fresh; 6. dis color; 7. in complete; 8. re search; 9. un happy; 10. dis connect; 11. re tell

Page 9: 1. useless; 2. restless; 3. goodness; 4. fruitless; 5. likeness;

Page 10: 1. completely; 2. carefully; 3. hopeless; 4. cloudless; 5. motionless; 6. lightly; 7. quickly; 8. senseless; 9. swiftly; 10. restless; 11. entirely; 12. highly; 13. rapidly; 14. slowly; 15. neatly

Page 11: Words with the suffix "less": homeless; odorless; colorless; harmless; hopeless; careless; sleepless; helpless Words with the suffix "ness": sweetness; loneliness; happiness; softness; sadness; neatness; goodness; sickness

Page 12: neatly, neatness; likely, likeness; happily, happiness; sickly, sickness; hardly, hardness

Page 13: 1. laughable; 2. enjoyable; 3. wearable; 4. agreeable, 5. drinkable; 6. readable; 7. trainable

Page 14: 1. bat; 2. sing; 3. jog; 4. hit; 5. pop; 6. call; 7. ski; 8. bake; 9. shop; 10. walk; 11. drum; 12. hunt; 13. dig

Page 15: 1. play; 2. act; 3. watch; 4. cook; 5. cry; 6. dry; 7. jump; 8. place; 9. rule; 10. race; 11. wag; 12. flip; 13. push; 14. slam

Page 16: 1. trotted; 2. juggled; 3. jumped; 4. liked; 5. touched; 6. yelled; 7. walked; 8. grinned; 9. jogged; 10. napped; 11. drummed; 12. crushed; 13. rained

Page 17: 1. hopping; 2. sitting; 3. yelling; 4. getting; 5. trotting; 6. dripping; 7. running; 8. fanning

A

Page 19: 1. skat<u>ing</u>; 2. fad<u>ing</u>; 3. mak<u>ing</u>; 4. driv<u>ing</u>; 5. rid<u>ing</u>; 6. clos<u>ing</u>; 7. sav<u>ing</u>; 8. bak<u>ing</u>; 9. tak<u>ing</u>; 10. hop<u>ing</u>; 11. trac<u>ing</u>; 12. nam<u>ing</u>

Page 20: Top of page: A. <u>re</u>read; B. <u>re</u>fill; C. <u>re</u>build; D. <u>re</u>write; E. <u>re</u>call; F. <u>mis</u>spell; G. <u>mis</u>behave; H. <u>pre</u>heat or <u>re</u>heat; I. <u>re</u>new; J. <u>re</u>seal; K. <u>pre</u>school; L. <u>mis</u>lead Bottom of page: 1. refill; 2. reread; 3. mislead; 4. renew; 5. reseal; 6. rewrite; 7. misbehave; 8. misspell; 9. rebuild

Page 21: The following words should be colored red: 1. jump/jumping; 2. hop/hopping 5. look/looking; 6. hug/hugging; 8. walk/walking; 9. camp/camping; 11. eat/eating; 12. swim/swimming; 13. shop/shopping; 15. dig/digging; 16. beg/begging

Page 22: Top of page: A. <u>un</u>usual; B. <u>dis</u>agree; C. <u>dis</u>continue; D. <u>de</u>frost; E. <u>un</u>safe; F. <u>un</u>lock; G. <u>dis</u>honest; H. <u>un</u>even; I. <u>un</u>true Bottom of page: 1. defrost; 2. unsafe; 3. unlock; 4. discontinue; 5. dishonest; 6. untrue; 7. disagree; 8. uneven; 9. unlock; 10. unusual

Page 23: 1. care<u>less</u>; 2. sad<u>ness</u>; 3. use<u>less</u>; 4. neat<u>ness</u>; 5. soft<u>ness</u>; 6. rest<u>less</u>; 7. hard<u>ness</u>; 8. home<u>less</u>; 9. hope<u>less</u>; 10. dark<u>ness</u>; 11. thank<u>less</u>; 12. good<u>ness</u>; 13. quick<u>ness</u>; 14. sad<u>ness</u>; 15. thought<u>less</u>; 16. shy<u>ness</u>

Page 24: Top of page: A. enjoy<u>able</u>; B. near<u>ly</u>; C. move<u>able</u>; D. thank<u>ful</u>; E. safe<u>ly</u>; F. pain<u>ful</u>; G. help<u>ful</u>; H. drink<u>able</u>; I. care<u>ful</u> Bottom of page: 1. moveable; 2. thankful; 3. painful; 4. nearly; 5. safely; 6. helpful; 7. drinkable; 8. careful; 9. enjoyable; 10. painful; 11. safely

Page 25: 1. want<u>ed</u>; 2. sav<u>ed</u>; 3. snow<u>ed</u>; 4. lik<u>ed</u>; 5. us<u>ed</u>; 6. talk<u>ed</u>; 7. wip<u>ed</u>; 8. bak<u>ed</u>; 9. shar<u>ed</u>; 10. burn<u>ed</u>; 11. fill<u>ed</u>; 12. mail<u>ed</u>; 13. rain<u>ed</u>

Page 26: Top of page: These words should be colored blue: B. hiking; D. riding; E. taking; F. raking Bottom of page: 1. going; 2. hiking; 3. looking; 4. raking; 5. standing; 6. sailing; 7. taking; 8. riding

Page 27: These words should be colored red: 1. carry/carried; 5. study/studied; 6. empty/emptied; 7. hurry/hurried; 9. marry/married; 12. worry/worried; 14. fry/fried; 15. try/tried; 16. copy/copied

Page 28: The following words should be circled: 1. camping; 2. packed; 3. hunt; 4. picked; 5. splashing; 6. pulled; 7. filled; 8. rest; 9. fishing; 10. end

Page 29: 1. knock<u>ed</u>; 2. fish<u>ing</u>; 3. camp<u>ing</u>; 4. dish<u>ing</u>; 5. hunt<u>ing</u>; 6. toss<u>ed</u>

Page 30: 1. jogg<u>ed</u>; 2. cross<u>ing</u>; 3. batt<u>ing</u>; 4. skin<u>ned</u>; 5. kick<u>ed</u>; 6. stopp<u>ing</u>; 7. grin<u>ning</u>; 8. trott<u>ed</u>; 9. walk<u>ing</u>; 10. jump<u>ed</u>; 11. wash<u>ed</u>; 12. open<u>ing</u>; 13. play<u>ing</u>; 14. call<u>ing</u>

Page 31: 1. lift<u>ed</u>; 2. shopp<u>ing</u>; 3. dripp<u>ing</u>; 4. rush<u>ing</u>; 5. splash<u>ing</u>; 6. sobb<u>ed</u>; 7. run<u>ning</u>; 8. tripp<u>ed</u>; 9. call<u>ed</u>; 10. clapp<u>ed</u>; 11. rais<u>ed</u>

Page 32: Words that have no changes to the base word: 1. stamping; 2. sorting; 3. fussing; 4. squinting; 5. playing; 6. catching. Words with the final consonant doubled: 1. humming; 2. dragging; 3. wrapping; 4. slamming; 5. running; 6. swimming. Words that have the silent "e" dropped: 1. skating, 2. tasting; 3. braking; 4. joking; 5. sliding; 6. wiping

Page 33: 1. asking, camping, darting 2. hitting, clapping, humming 3. smiling, skating, saving 4. wanting, twisting, turning 5. popping, swimming, rubbing 6. tagging, wrapping, setting

Page 34: 1. unbutton; 2. uncover; 3. untrue; 4. unable; 5. uneasy; 6. undress; 7. unknown; 8. unfold; 9. untidy; 10. uneven; 11. untie; 12. unusual

Page 35: Word List: unwelcome, untie, unusual, uncover, undress, uneven, unbutton, untidy, unclean, unfold, uneasy, unknown

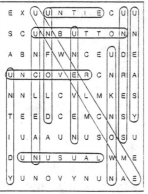

Page 36: 1. rewrite; 2. reread; 3. reheat; 4. rejoin; 5. rebuild; 6. return; 7. recite; 8. rehang; 9. renew; 10. reword; 11. refuel; 12. refill

Page 37: Word List: refuel, rehang, recite, rejoin, reword, refill, rebuild, reheat, renew, redo, rewrite, reread

Page 37 (cont.):

Page 38: 1. preteen; 2. presoak; 3. preschool; 4. pretest; 5. precook; 6. preschool; 7. preshrunk; 8. prepaid; 9. prehistoric; 10. preview; 11. pretest; 12. Preheat

Page 39: Word List: prepay, preview, presoak, preheat, prepaid, preshrunk, preschool, prehistoric, pretest, preteen, precook, precaution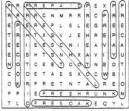

Page 40: 1. prefix; 2. unable; 3. preshrunk; 4. renew; 5. unsure; 6. prejudge; 7. refill; 8. unsafe; 9. untrue; 10. unwilling

Page 41: 1. unbutton; 2. recite; 3. preschool; 4. relocate; 5. refund; 6. rebuild; 7. unhappy; 8. preheat; 9. rewind; 10. pretest; 11. restore; 12. refill; 13. renew; 14. unfold; 15. unload

Page 42: 1. prehistoric; 2. retrace; 3. return; 4. reunion; 5. unable; 6. replace; 7. unbearable; 8. reclaim; 9. review or preview; 10. reread

Page 43: 1. automobile; 2. television; 3. telephone; 4. midnight; 5. midair; 6. telegraph; 7. midpoint; 8. midsummer; 9. telescope

Page 44:

```
P R E V I E W D W X T
C T M I D C R S U K E
S T E L E P H O N E P
R U N D I F C O A L R
E C M I D A I R B V E
W T R S Y Z M O L I P
A E P R E P A Y E E L
R B O M G I H T P X A
D I L M D P S W R A C
M I D P O I N T E N E
R E S M I D N I G H T
U N L I K E L T F G Y
```

Page 45: 1. The second bird is **shorter** the other. 2. The **fattest** dog has spots. 3. The soup is **hotter** than the drink. 4. The **tallest** boy is wearing a cap.

Page 46: The following words should be circled: 1. biggest; 2. tallest; 3. faster; 4. higher; 5. cutest; 6. cleaner; 7. shortest; 8. hungrier; 9. easier; 10. louder; 11. slowest; 12. heavier; 13. tallest; 14. youngest; 15. prettiest; 16. smaller; 17. hardest

Page 47: The following words should be circled: 1. sweeter; 2. nicest; 3. friendliest; 4. riper; 5. lighter; 6. hottest; 7. deeper; 8. closest; 9. nicest; 10. funniest; 11. colder; 12. louder; 13. fastest

Page 48: Across: 1. pretest; 3. preschool; 5. repaint; 6. unlock Down: 2. recycle; 3. preteen; 4. unbutton

Page 49: 1. untie; 2. repay; 3. unpack; 4. recall; 5. redo; 6. replace; 7. recite; 8. unlock; 9. telephone; 10. autographed; 11. disagree; 12. inside; 13. misprint; 14. disappoint; 15. misspell; 16. repaint

Page 50: 1. re fresh ment; 2. un depend able; 3. en large ment; 4. re new able; 5. dis approve ing; 6. un truth ful; 7. pre arrange ment; 8. un touch able; 9. re finish ed; 10. re turn able; 11. de light ful; 12. un willing ness; 13. en list ing; 14. in dispense able; 15. dis grace ful

Page 51: untie; preschool; unglue; prepay; uneven; presoak; unclear; preshrunk

Page 53: Answers will vary.

Page 54: Words in these areas should be colored red: friendly, softly, slowly, highly, rapidly. Words in these areas should be colored orange: sickness, neatness. Words in these areas should be colored purple: helpless, priceless. Words in these areas shoud be colored blue: freshen, darken, shorten.

Page 55: Answers will vary.

Page 56: 1. unlock; 2. unpack; 3. inside; 4. unwrap; 5. untie; 6. telephone; 7. midnight; 8. automobile

Page 57: 1. baker; 2. singing; 3. whistling; 4. crying; 5. napping; 6. skating; 7. jogger; 8. painting

Page 58: 1. scrubbing; 2. begged; 3. grinning; 4. rushed; 5. dressed; 6. dripping; 7. matching; 8. trotted; 9. jogging; 10. hemmed; 11. napping; 12. zipped; 13. painted

Page 59: 1. rewrite, write; 2. unsure, sure; 3. washing, wash; 4. unhappy, happy; 5. reread, read; 6. jumping, jump; 7. evenly, even; 8. misuse, use; 9. preshrunk, shrunk; 10. plowed, plow; 11. kindness, kind; 12. uneven, even; 13. hanging, hang; 14. teacher, teach

Page 60: 1. re – view; 2. un – pack; 3. re – design; 4. dis – agree – able; 5. enjoy – able; 6. un – teach – able; 7. un – believe– able; 8. dis – appoint – ment; 9. swift – ly

D

Complete each sentence by adding the correct suffix to the word in parentheses.

1. The crowd cheered as the man _____ the weights. **(lift)**

2. My father is taking me _____ for new tennis shoes. **(shop)**

3. The water was _____ from the faucet. **(drip)**

4. People were _____ to get their tickets for the basketball game. **(rush)**

5. Water was _____ as the swimmers swam across the pool. **(splash)**

6. Cindy, who is a very poor sport, _____ because her team didn't win the game. **(sob)**

7. The football team was _____ laps around the track. **(run)**

8. Katie _____ over her shoelace because it was untied. **(trip)**

9. My sister told me that Susan _____ me last night. **(call)**

10. Sally's family _____ and cheered when she hit a home run. **(clap)**

11. The teacher chose Emily because she _____ her hand first. **(raise)**

Read the words in the word list. Think about what changes need to be made before adding "ing." Write the new words in the correct columns.

No changes to base word	Double the final consonant	Drop the silent "e"
1. _____	1. _____	1. _____
2. _____	2. _____	2. _____
3. _____	3. _____	3. _____
4. _____	4. _____	4. _____
5. _____	5. _____	5. _____
6. _____	6. _____	6. _____

BUSY BEE
HONEY

Word List

skate	hum	taste	drag	wrap	stamp
sort	slam	fuss	brake	squint	joke
run	play	catch	swim	slide	wipe

In each tic-tac-toe frame, circle three words in a row that would have the suffix "ing" added in the same manner.

1.

chase	bake	hop
jog	paint	roast
ask	camp	dart

2.

beg	hike	joke
hit	clap	hum
kick	jump	bike

3.

race	smile	last
rest	skate	pave
place	save	set

4.

want	twist	turn
mop	behave	talk
live	sort	nod

5.

place	time	rip
pop	swim	rub
bake	pack	land

6.

jump	tag	amuse
vote	wrap	use
waste	set	boss

33

Correctly complete the sentences by adding the prefix "un" to the words in the word list. Use the new words to finish the sentences below.

Word List					
____known	____easy	____true	____button	____tie	____fold
____cover	____tidy	____usual	____dress	____even	____able

1. My baby brother learned how to _____ his shirt today.

2. The dog was digging in the dirt to _____ the bones he'd buried.

3. The rumor about Jamaal moving was _____ .

4. Juan was _____ to go to the game because he was on vacation.

5. Dan felt _____ about having the dentist pull his tooth.

6. Mary's little sister loves to dress and _____ her doll.

7. The story was written by an _____ author.

8. _____ the napkin before putting it on your lap.

9. My father is unhappy because Jordan keeps his room so _____ .

10. The hem of my dress was _____ until the tailor fixed it.

11. Don't take off your tennis shoes unless you _____ the laces first.

12. My friend Bobby has a very

_____

pet—a skunk!

Add the prefix "un" to each word in the word list. Then find and circle the words in the puzzle below. The words are spelled down, across, and diagonally.

Word List					
____welcome	____tie	____usual	____cover	____dress	____even
____button	____tidy	____clean	____fold	____easy	____known

```
E  X  U  U  N  T  I  E  C  U  U
S  C  U  N  B  U  T  T  O  N  N
A  B  N  F  W  N  C  E  U  D  E
U  N  C  O  V  E  R  C  N  R  A
N  N  L  L  C  V  L  M  K  E  S
T  E  E  D  C  E  M  C  N  S  Y
I  U  A  A  U  N  U  S  O  S  U
D  U  N  U  S  U  A  L  W  M  E
Y  U  N  O  V  Y  N  U  N  A  E
```

Correctly complete the sentences by adding the prefix "re" to each word in the word list.

Word List

____word   ____hang   ____cite   ___ join   ____fuel   ____turn

____build   ____heat   ____new   ____fill   ____write   ____read

---

1. Teresa didn't hand in a neat report, so the teacher asked her to _____ it.

2. If you _____ the story, I think you will understand it better.

3. My father will _____ the cold pizza so it will taste better.

4. Mike enjoyed the hiking club, so he decided to _____ this year.

5. The farmer had to _____ his barn after it burned down.

6. I must _____ these books to the library by Saturday.

7. Candy is going to _____ a poem she has memorized.

8. Take the picture down and _____ it a little higher.

9. I am not finished reading this book, so I will _____ it at the library.

10. Please _____ the directions so they are clear.

11. The airplane had to _____ at the airport before taking off.

12. I must _____ my hamster's water bottle with fresh water every day.

36

Add the prefix "re" to the words in the word list to make new words. Then find and circle the new words in the puzzle below. The words are spelled across, down, and diagonally.

Word List

____fuel   ____hang   ____cite   ____join   ____word   ____fill

____build   ____heat   ____new   ____do   ____write   ____read

WORD BUILDERS

```
R  R  E  F  U  E  L  R  Y  T
E  R  E  R  E  A  D  E  R  R
U  E  E  H  E  C  N  C  E  E
R  H  C  B  A  W  U  I  W  W
E  E  C  N  U  N  R  T  O  R
J  A  N  E  R  I  G  E  R  I
O  T  R  E  F  I  L  L  D  T
I  R  E  C  W  B  N  D  W  E
N  E  C  M  P  E  R  E  D  O
```

37

Complete the sentences by adding the prefix "pre" to each word in the word list.

Word List

_____soak   _____view   _____test   _____heat   _____cook

_____shrunk   _____paid   _____teen   _____school   _____historic

---

1. Paul is a teenager, but his twelve-year-old sister is a _____ .

2. The stain will come out if you _____ the shirt before you wash it.

3. My three-year-old sister is starting _____ this fall.

4. The spelling _____ was today, but the final test is on Friday.

5. Please _____ the potatoes so they will be ready to eat for dinner.

6. Many children go to _____ before they go to kindergarten.

7. Blue jeans that are _____ won't shrink when they are washed.

8. Our circus tickets are _____ because we bought them early.

9. In science class, we learned that dinosaurs were _____ .

10. We saw the_____ for the movie before anyone else did.

11. The teacher gave the class a _____ to see how much they knew.

12. _____ the oven before you bake the pie.

Complete the sentences by adding the prefix "pre" to the words in the word list. Then find and circle the words in the puzzle below. The words are spelled across, down, and diagonally.

Word List

____pay	____view	____soak	____heat	____paid	____shrunk
____school	____historic	____test	____teen	____cook	____caution

```
P  R  P  R  E  P  A  I  D  P  E  X  P  P
R  R  R  R  C  N  M  R  R  R  C  P  R  R
E  P  E  R  E  P  L  S  L  E  G  R  E  E
T  R  H  T  X  S  V  J  E  H  R  E  P  C
E  E  I  E  E  S  C  N  I  E  A  V  A  A
E  C  S  H  T  S  N  H  X  A  V  I  Y  U
N  O  T  C  E  E  T  C  O  T  N  E  D  T
C  O  O  E  T  A  E  S  X  O  C  W  B  I
O  K  R  P  R  E  T  N  T  A  L  R  E  O
P  P  I  E  P  R  E  S  H  R  U  N  K  N
T  L  C  P  R  E  S  O  A  K  E  Q  Y  L
```

39

Add the prefix "un," "re," or "pre" to the words in the word list and use them to correctly complete the sentences below.

Word List				
_____true	_____shrunk	_____sure	_____fill	_____fix
_____willing	_____safe	_____judge	_____new	_____able

un + safe

1. The **un** in **unsafe** is a _____ .

2. He was _____ to lift the heavy weight.

3. His pants were not _____ so they were too tight after he washed them.

4. The library book was due, but Jim was able to _____ it.

5. Jeff was _____ of what to do.

6. If you _____ people, you are forming an opinion about them before you know them.

7. Please _____ all of the glasses with iced tea.

8. It is _____ to swim in that lake.

9. People once thought the world was flat, but that was _____ .

10. His father was _____ to hear his excuse.

**Add either "un," "re," or "pre" to the words in the word list to make new words.
Use the words to correctly complete the sentences below.**

Word List

_____store	_____happy	_____build	_____fund	_____school
_____button	_____test	_____cite	_____wind	_____locate
_____fold	_____fill	_____load	_____new	_____heat

1. My little sister can _____ her own coat.

2. Annie will _____ a poem called "Ode to a Robin."

3. My little brother is not old enough for kindergarten, so he is in _____ .

4. The company will _____ to a different city next year.

5. The store will _____ your money if the toy doesn't work.

6. The storm destroyed our playhouse, so we had to _____ it.

7. Vicki was _____ because she got a "C" on her test.

8. Before baking the cake, we must _____ the oven.

9. Please _____ the video tape before returning it to the store.

10. Mitch's class has a spelling _____ every Monday morning.

11. The museum planned to _____ the oil paintings.

12. I spilled the bucket of water, so I had to _____ it.

13. I had to _____ the books I checked out of the library.

14. Please _____ the tablecloth so I can put it on the table.

15. I helped Rick _____ the boxes from the truck.

Write the prefix "un," "re," or "pre" in each blank to form a new word.

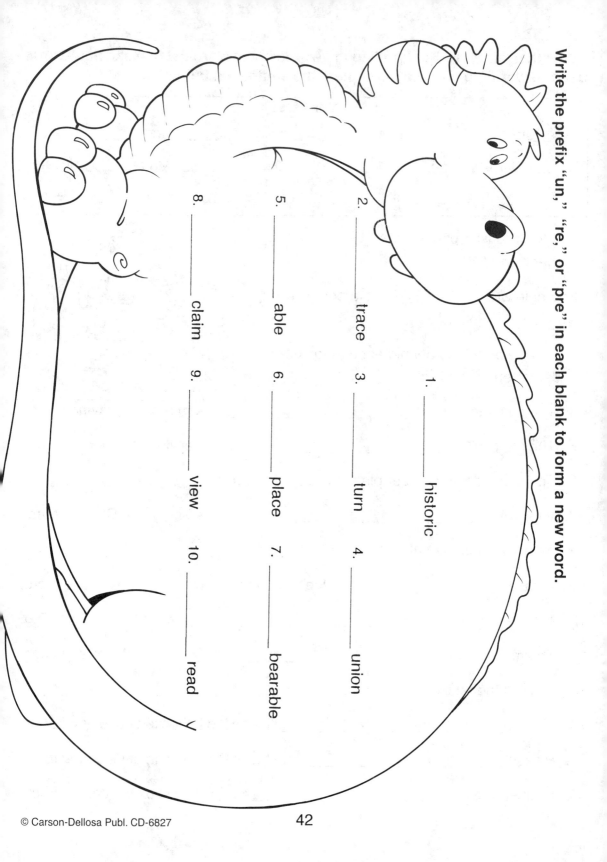

1. _____ historic

2. _____ trace

3. _____ turn

4. _____ union

5. _____ able

6. _____ place

7. _____ bearable

8. _____ claim

9. _____ view

10. _____ read

Write the prefix "tele," "mid," or "auto" in each blank to form a new word.

The prefix **tele** means **"distant."**   The prefix **mid** means **"middle."**
The prefix **auto** means **"self."**

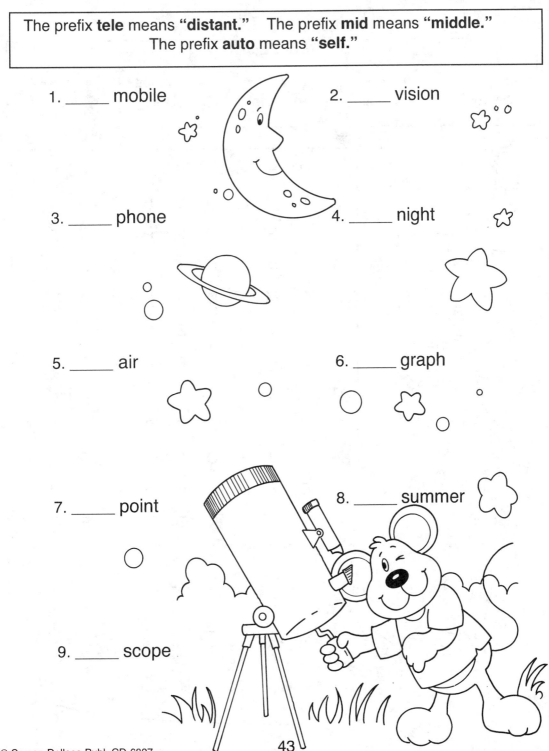

1. _____ mobile

2. _____ vision

3. _____ phone

4. _____ night

5. _____ air

6. _____ graph

7. _____ point

8. _____ summer

9. _____ scope

43

Find and circle each word in the puzzle below. The words are written down and across.

Word List

telephone	unable	reward	midnight	preview
prepay	replace	midpoint	unlike	midair

P R E V I E W D W X T
C T M I D C R S U K E
S T E L E P H O N E P
R U N D I F C O A L R
E C M I D A I R B V E
W T R S Y Z M O L I P
A E P R E P A Y E E L
R B O M G I H T P X A
D I L M D P S W R A C
M I D P O I N T E N E
R E S M I D N I G H T
U N L I K E L T F G Y

Circle the correct word for each sentence. Remember to use the suffix "er" when comparing two things. Use the suffix "est" when comparing more than two things.

1. The second bird is **(shorter, shortest)** than the other.

2. The **(fattest, fatter)** dog has spots.

3. The soup is **(hotter, hottest)** than the drink.

4. The **(tallest, taller)** boy is wearing a cap.

Read each sentence and circle the correct word.

1. Her dog is the **(bigger, biggest)** one in the pet show.

2. That oak tree is the **(tallest, taller)** tree in our yard.

3. John can type **(faster, fastest)** on his computer than Randy.

4. Cindy's kite can fly **(highest, higher)** than mine.

5. Susan has the **(cutest, cuter)** kitten I have ever seen.

6. Stephanie's room was **(cleanest, cleaner)** than Pat's room.

7. Zachary is the **(shortest, shorter)** boy in our class.

8. Jamaal ate all of his lunch. He was **(hungrier, hungriest)** than George.

9. Amanda thought this test was **(easier, easiest)** than the first one.

10. The lunch bell sounded **(louder, loudest)** than the recess bell.

11. Teresa knew she was the **(slowest, slower)** runner when she finished tenth in the race.

12. Elizabeth lifted a box that was **(heavier, heaviest)** than mine.

13. The **(taller, tallest)** building I ever saw is in New York City.

14. Cindy was the **(youngest, younger)** girl in her family.

15. Mr. Sanders has the **(prettiest, prettier)** roses in his garden.

16. Tina's bedroom is **(smaller, smallest)** than Tracy's bedroom.

17. The last problem on the math test was the **(harder, hardest)** one.

Read each sentence and circle the correct word.

1. My watermelon is **(sweeter, sweetest)** than Peter's lemon.

2. Mr. Owens is the **(nicer, nicest)** teacher in our school.

3. Megan's dog is the **(friendlier, friendliest)** one on our block.

4. The peaches were **(riper, ripest)** than the bananas.

5. My spring jacket is **(lighter, lightest)** than my winter coat.

6. Yesterday was the **(hotter, hottest)** day of the summer.

7. One end of the swimming pool was **(deeper, deepest)** than the other end.

8. Of all the children in my class, I live the **(closest, closer)** to the school.

9. Marcy is the **(nicest, nicer)** person on my soccer team.

10. The comedian had the **(funnier, funniest)** act in the show.

11. The ice cream was **(colder, coldest)** than the cake after we put in the freezer.

12. The thunder made a **(louder, loudest)** sound than the pouring rain.

13. Jerry built the **(faster, fastest)** model airplane.

Use the words from the word list to complete the crossword puzzle.

Word List
unlock
preschool
pretest
unbutton
preteen
repaint
recycle

Across:
1. The teacher gave us a _____ to see how much we knew.

3. My three-year-old sister goes to _____.

5. I have to _____ the fence every summer.

6. Use your key to _____ the door.

Down:
2. My family has to _____ all our newspapers.

3. A 10- to 12-year-old person is a _____.

4. Tim had to _____ his coat so he could put on his scarf.

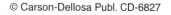

Read each sentence. Circle the prefix in each bold word.

1. I could not **u n t i e** my shoelace because of the knot.

2. We had to **r e p a y** our neighbor for the window we accidentally broke.

3. Sarah went upstairs to **u n p a c k** her suitcase.

4. Do you **r e c a l l** our new teacher's name?

5. I had to **r e d o** my homework because I did not understand the assignment

6. The toy store offered to **r e p l a c e** the toys that were broken.

7. Tom had to **r e c i t e** the poem to the class.

8. Please **u n l o c k** the door and let the dog into the house.

9. Please answer the **t e l e p h o n e** if it rings.

10. Mike had an **a u t o g r a p h e d** picture of the famous actor.

11. My sister and I **d i s a g r e e** about who should walk the dog.

12. Tom and Jeremy are waiting for us **i n s i d e**.

13. The newspaper article contained a **m i s p r i n t**.

14. Please do not **d i s a p p o i n t** Juan by not going to his party.

15. I did not **m i s s p e l l** any words on my spelling test this week!

16. I decided to **r e p a i n t** the chair because I did not like the color.

Try to divide the words below by separating the prefixes, suffixes, and base words. The first one is done for you.

Remember: Sometimes the silent **e** is removed from the base word when a suffix is added.

Example: remove — removable

	Prefix	Base Word	Suffix
1. refreshment	re	fresh	ment
2. undependable			
3. enlargement			
4. renewable			
5. disapproving			
6. untruthful			
7. prearrangement			
8. untouchable			
9. refinished			
10. returnable			
11. delightful			
12. unwillingness			
13. enlisting			
14. indispensable			
15. disgraceful			

Read the word on each spade. Paste the base word next to the correct prefix.

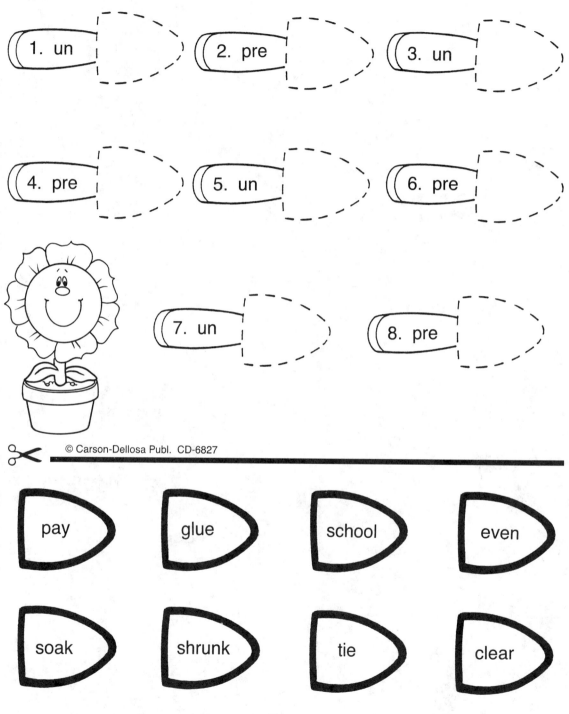

1. un

2. pre

3. un

4. pre

5. un

6. pre

7. un

8. pre

pay

glue

school

even

soak

shrunk

tie

clear

Try to write the definitions for the words below in your own words. The box at the bottom of the page will help you. You many use a dictionary if you need to.

1. precooked _____

2. unsure _____

3. rewind _____

4. colorless _____

5. brownish _____

6. sickness _____

7. friendly _____

8. presoak _____

9. disappear _____

Below is a list of the meanings of some prefixes and suffixes.

PREFIXES	SUFFIXES
re— back or again	**ment**— the act, result or product of
dis—away, apart, the opposite of	**ness**— condition, quality, or state of being
un— opposite, not or lack of	**ish**— like or about
pre— before	**ly**— like or as
	less— without or not

Use the key to color the puzzle.

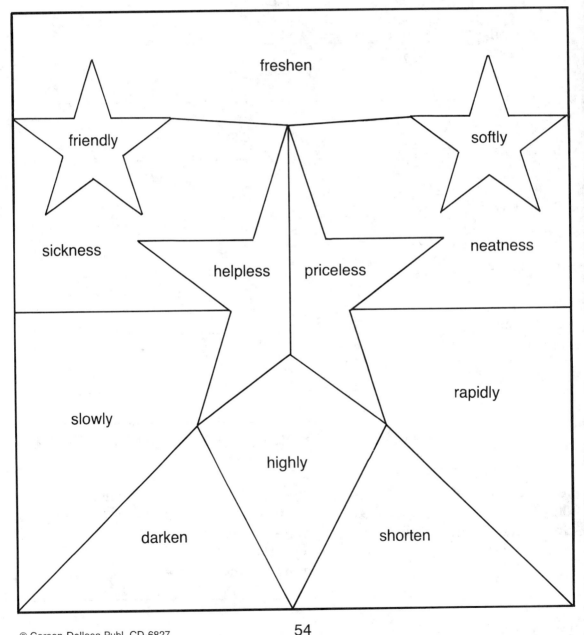

freshen

friendly

softly

sickness

helpless priceless

neatness

slowly

rapidly

highly

darken

shorten

**Write a sentence about each animal.
Use the words in the word list.**

Word List

longest
fattest
smallest
tallest
heaviest
shortest
thinnest

1. _____

_____

2. _____

_____

3. _____

_____

4. _____

_____

Circle the word that matches each picture.

1. unload
   unlock
   unsafe

2. unhappy
   unpack
   uncut

3. inside
   input
   indirect

4. unwrap
   unglue
   unbutton

5. unpack
   untie
   unclear

6. telegraph
   telescope
   telephone

7. midair
   midnight
   midpoint

8. autograph
   autobiography
   automobile

Circle the word that matches each picture.

1. baker

   cleaner

   grocer

5. naming

   nodding

   napping

2. singing

   standing

   sliding

6. skating

   shutting

   screaming

3. whistling

   walking

   waiting

7. teacher

   jogger

   cycler

4. cooking

   crying

   cleaning

8. painting

   scrubbing

   washing

57

Complete the sentences by adding either "ing" or "ed" to the words from the word list. Use the words to complete the sentences below.

Word List						
hem___	beg_____	paint___	zip___	jog___	dress___	drip___
grin___	march___	match___	nap___	rush___	scrub___	trot___

1. Sean was _____ the frying pan at the kitchen sink.

2. Susan _____ her mother to let her keep the kitten.

3. Betsy was _____ from ear to ear when she was given the award.

4. Because we were late, Mandy and I _____ to catch the bus this morning.

5. Tim got _____ up to go to the party.

6. The bathroom faucet was _____ all night long.

7. My brother loves to play _____ games with his cards.

8. The race horse _____ around the track.

9. Dad has been _____ every morning since he started a diet.

10. Zach's new pants were too long, so he had them _____ .

11. The baby has been_____for over two hours.

12. Ben_____ up his sleeping bag to help keep him warm.

13. Anthony and I _____ the doghouse this afternoon.

Read the words. Circle the prefix or suffix in each word. Write the base word on the line.

Base Word

1. r e w r i t e   _____

2. u n s u r e   _____

3. w a s h i n g   _____

4. u n h a p p y   _____

5. r e r e a d   _____

6. j u m p i n g   _____

7. e v e n l y   _____

8. m i s u s e   _____

9. p r e s h r u n k   _____

10. p l o w e d   _____

11. k i n d n e s s   _____

12. u n e v e n   _____

13. h a n g i n g   _____

14. t e a c h e r   _____

Rewrite the words on the lines. Draw a line between the prefix or suffix and the base word.

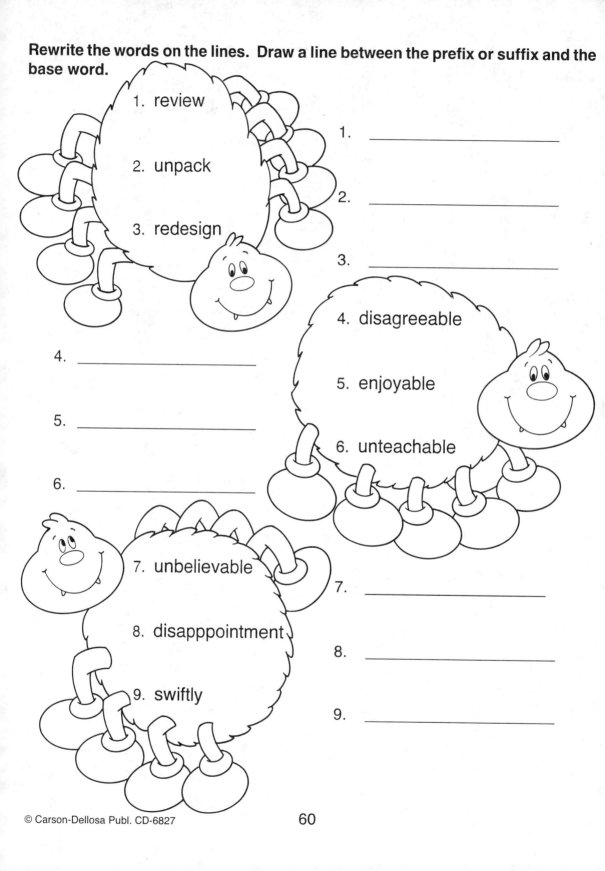

1. review

2. unpack

3. redesign

1. _____

2. _____

3. _____

4. disagreeable

5. enjoyable

6. unteachable

4. _____

5. _____

6. _____

7. unbelievable

8. disapppointment

9. swiftly

7. _____

8. _____

9. _____